LIFE CYCLES

The
Ladybug

Published by Raintree Steck-Vaughn Publishers, an imprint of Steck-Vaughn Company.

Acknowledgments
Project Editor: Helene Resky
Design Manager: Joyce Spicer
Consulting Editor: Kim Merlino
Consultant: Michael Chinery
Illustrated: Jim Chanell
Designed by Ian Winton and Steve Prosser
Electronic Cover Production: Alan Klemp
Additional Electronic Production: Bo McKinney and Scott Melcer
Photography credits on page 32

Planned and produced by The Creative Publishing Company

Library of Congress Cataloging-in-Publication Data
Crewe, Sabrina
The ladybug / Sabrina Crewe.
p. cm. — (Life cycles)
Includes index.
Summary: Describes the life cycle, habitat, and eating habits of the seven-spotted ladybug and similar beetles.
ISBN 0-8172-4366-6 (hardcover). — ISBN 0-8172-6229-6 (pbk.)
1. Ladybugs — Juvenile literature.   2. Seven-spotted ladybug — Juvenile literature.
3. Ladybugs — Life cycles — Juvenile literature.   4. Seven-spotted ladybug — Life cycles — Juvenile literature.   [1. Ladybugs.   2. Beetles.]   I. Title.   II. Series: Crewe, Sabrina. Life cycles.
QL596.C65C74   1997
595.76'9 — dc20   96-4830
                                               CIP   AC

    4 5 6 7 8 9 0 LB 00
Printed and bound in the United States of America.

Words explained in the glossary appear in
bold the first time they are used in the text.

The
Ladybug

Sabrina Crewe

RAINTREE
STECK-VAUGHN
PUBLISHERS

A Harcourt Company

Austin • New York
www.steck-vaughn.com

The eggs are on the leaf.

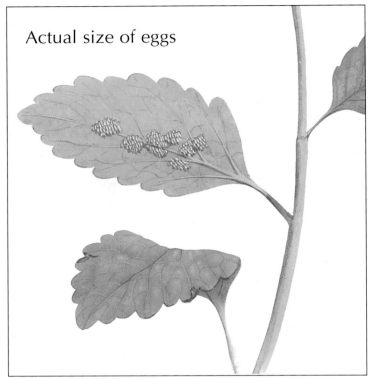

Actual size of eggs

A ladybug has laid its eggs on
a leaf. The tiny eggs are warmed
by the sun.

The larvae are hatching.

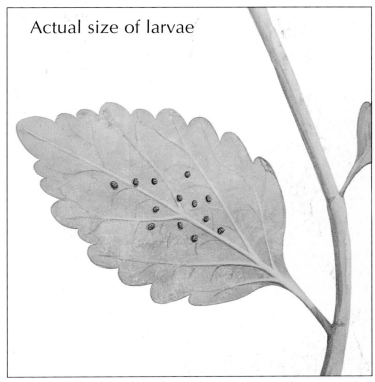

Actual size of larvae

After a few days, the eggs open. The
ladybug **larvae** come out. They look
like caterpillars with six legs. The
larvae are very small when they **hatch**.

The larva has a strong mouth.

Larvae feed on **aphids** that they find on leaves. They squeeze the aphids in their mouths and eat the insides. The larva eats many aphids in a day and grows quickly.

The larva climbs out of its skin.

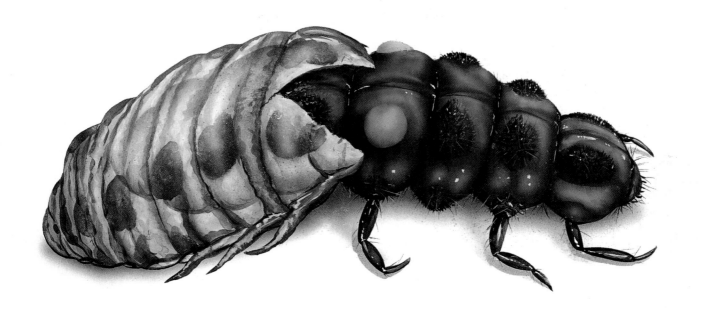

As the larva gets bigger, its skin becomes too tight. The skin splits, and the larva climbs out. Now it has a new, looser skin.

The larva is fully grown.

The larva is four weeks old. It has
changed its skin three times. The larva
sticks itself to a leaf stem. It is ready
to change into something new.

The larva becomes a pupa.

The larva's skin has rolled back. Under this skin is a different kind of skin. Now the larva has changed into a **pupa**.

The pupa is resting.

The skin of the pupa has become
hard. It protects the creature inside.
The pupa hardly moves, but big
changes are happening inside its skin.

A new animal is forming.

Let's look inside at the pupa. Its body is becoming smaller. Its head is growing, and its legs are getting longer. You can see wings and **antennae** starting to grow.

A ladybug is coming out.

After eight days, a new ladybug has formed.
It is ready to come out. The ladybug pushes
its way out of the pupa skin.

The ladybug spreads its new wings.

At first the ladybug's wings are soft
and wet. The ladybug dries them
in the sun. It stays very still until the
wings have become hard.

The ladybug is turning red!

As the wings dry, the ladybug's wing
cases change color and get their spots.
The wing cases get hard as they turn red.
They form a shell over the back wings.

The ladybug is taking off.

The ladybug's wing cases are its front wings. When the ladybug wants to fly, it lifts the wing cases and beats its back wings.

The ladybug waves its antennae.

The ladybug's antennae move as
it senses things around it. Ladybugs
use their antennae to touch and smell.
The antennae help the ladybug find food.

Ladybugs have a favorite food.

The adult ladybug feeds on aphids, just like it did when it was a larva. But now it munches the whole insect. Ladybugs eat other small insects and insect eggs, too.

The ladybug eats parts of flowers.

Sometimes the ladybug feeds on **nectar** and **pollen** made by flowers. Pollen sticks to the ladybug's body. When the ladybug visits another plant, the pollen may fall off. This helps the plant make seeds.

Ladybugs are useful.

Farmers and gardeners like ladybugs because they carry pollen from one flower to another and **prey** on insects that can hurt plants. Many farmers and gardeners buy ladybugs to live on their plants and eat other insects!

The ladybug is in danger.

The ladybug has been seen by an
assassin bug. Some large insects
and birds eat ladybugs, their eggs,
and their larvae.

Ladybugs taste horrible!

The bad smell and taste of ladybugs can help save them from some **predators**. Ladybugs protect themselves by curling up into their shells, too.

Winter is coming.

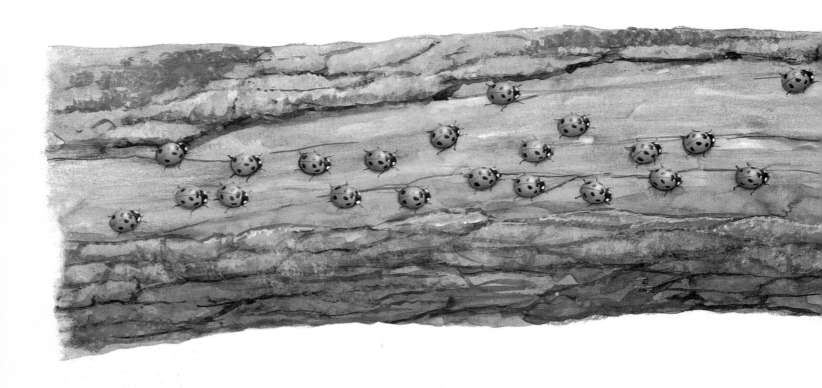

When it gets cold, there is no food
for ladybugs. They gather together
in large groups.

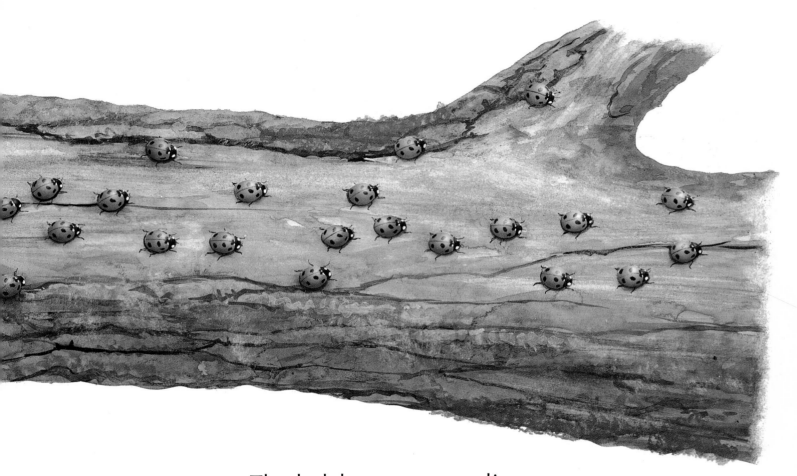

The ladybugs are crawling
along the tree in a line. They
are looking for somewhere
safe to spend the winter.

The ladybugs are hibernating.

The ladybugs have found a place to sleep. They do not move or eat. They will **hibernate** until it gets warm again.

The ladybug lays its eggs.

It is spring. The ladybugs have woken up. Ladybugs mate in spring to **fertilize** the eggs of the females. A week after mating, female ladybugs lay their eggs.

Parts of a Ladybug

Ladybugs are **beetles**. Beetles are a type of insect with front wings that make a hard cover over their back wings and bodies. Like all insects, they have six legs and a head, **thorax**, and **abdomen**.

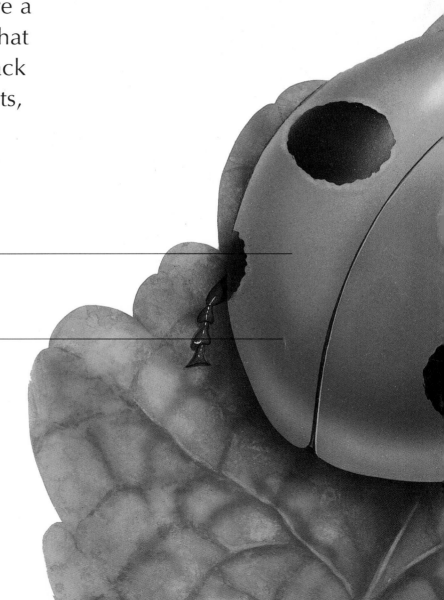

Color
Bright coloring warns enemies that ladybugs taste bad

Abdomen
Rear part of the body

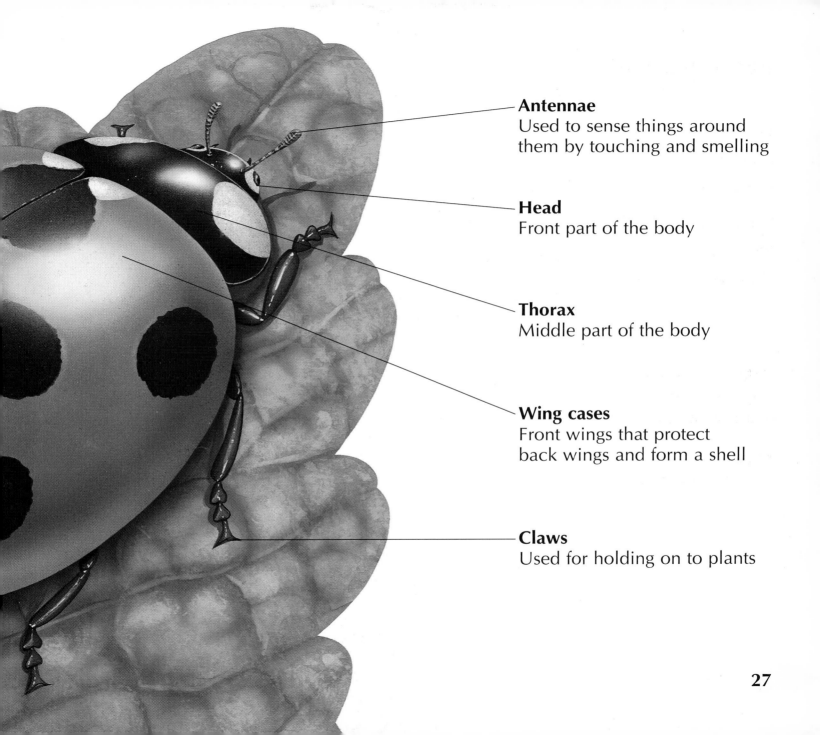

Antennae
Used to sense things around
them by touching and smelling

Head
Front part of the body

Thorax
Middle part of the body

Wing cases
Front wings that protect
back wings and form a shell

Claws
Used for holding on to plants

27

Other Beetles

The ladybug in this book
is a seven-spotted ladybug.
Here are some other ladybugs
and different kinds of beetles.

Rodolia cardinalis

Orange ladybug

American stag beetle

22-spotted ladybug

Rose curculio

Desert blister beetle

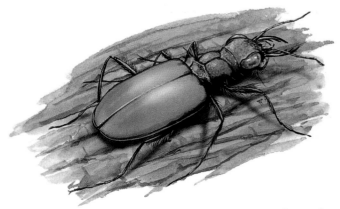

Splendid tiger beetle

Hairy bear beetle

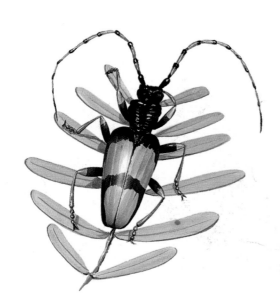

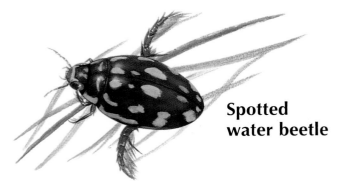

Spotted water beetle

Horse-bean longhorn

Where the Seven-Spotted Ladybug Lives

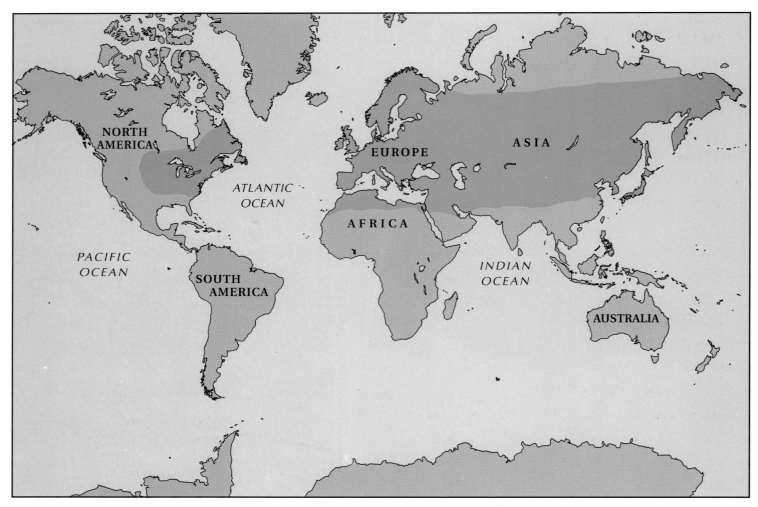

 Areas where the seven-spotted ladybug lives

Glossary

Abdomen The rear part of an insect's body

Antennae The feelers on an insect's head used to sense things around them

Aphid A small insect eaten by ladybugs

Beetle An insect with hard, shiny front wings that cover the back wings when resting

Fertilize To make a female's egg able to produce babies

Hatch To come out of an egg

Hibernate To spend the winter in a deep sleep

Larva The growing stage of an insect before it turns into a pupa. Plural is larvae

Nectar The sweet liquid made by flowers to attract insects

Pollen Tiny grains inside a flower that make seeds and fruit when they are carried to another flower

Predator An animal that hunts and kills other animals for food

Prey To hunt or kill another animal for food

Pupa The stage where an insect rests and changes into an adult. Plural is pupae

Thorax The middle part of an insect's body

Index

Photography credits

Front cover: (top left) Avril Ramage/Oxford Scientific Films; (middle left) Barrie Watts; (bottom left) Kim Taylor/Bruce Coleman; (right) Hans Reinhard/Bruce Coleman.

Title page: Andrew J. Purcell/Bruce Coleman; p. 4: Kim Taylor/Oxford Scientific Films; p. 5: Barrie Watts; p. 6: Neil Bromhall/Oxford Scientific Films; p. 8: Barrie Watts; p. 9: Kim Taylor/Bruce Coleman; p. 10: Barrie Watts; p. 12: Barrie Watts; p. 13: Jeremy Grayson/Bruce Coleman; p. 14: Avril Ramage/Oxford Scientific Films; p. 15: Kim Taylor/Bruce Coleman; p. 16: Andrew J. Purcell/Bruce Coleman; p. 17: Avril Ramage/Oxford Scientific Films; p. 18: Colin Milkins/Oxford Scientific Films; p. 19: Kim Taylor/Bruce Coleman; p. 21: Avril Ramage/Oxford Scientific Films; p. 24: Jane Burton/Bruce Coleman; p. 25: Avril Ramage/Oxford Scientific Films.